AF566876

the Devotional *for* WOMEN journal

NASHVILLE, TENNESSEE

When you come to God's Word with an open heart, ready to hear God speak, willing to respond to Him in obedience, you will find yourself in His story—your place in His master plan. He will teach you; He will conform you to His image; He will then use you in ways you could never have imagined except that you have spent time with Him! Let this journal be a friend to accompany you on your spiritual journey.

Rhonda Harrington Kelley
Dorothy Kelley Patterson

Printed in China

978-1-4627-4181-6

Published by B&H Publishing Group
Nashville, Tennessee

Dewey Decimal Classification: 242.2
Subject Heading: WOMEN \ SPIRITUAL LIFE \ DEVOTIONAL LITERATURE

1 2 3 4 5 6 7 8 • 22 21 20 19 18 17

New Life in Christ

Are you a Christian? A Christian is anyone who has received by faith the salvation God has provided in Jesus Christ. If you are a Christian, then you have new life in Christ here on earth and for all eternity.

Salvation is necessary because all have sinned against God (Rom. 3:23). Salvation begins with repentance—turning away from sin and turning toward God, who alone has the power to save. You cannot earn salvation by doing good works, for it is a gift of grace from God, accomplished through the death of His Son, Jesus Christ (Eph. 2:8–9). When Jesus died on the cross, He paid the price to forgive all sin (John 3:16; Rom. 5:8; 1 John 2:2). Romans 6:23 says, "For the wages of sin is death, but the gift of God is eternal life in Christ Jesus our Lord." God's free gift of salvation—the exchange of your sin for His righteousness—must be accepted by faith (Rom. 10:9–10). When you accept God's gift of salvation, you become a new creation (2 Cor. 5:17).

If you are a Christian, you are promised security in your salvation, but what is your present "new creation" life supposed to look like? What responsibilities do you have in maintaining a vibrant relationship with your Savior?

Your Christian life begins the moment you turn away from sin and, by faith, receive the salvation God has provided in the crucifixion and resurrection of His Son Jesus Christ. At that moment, the Holy Spirit makes Himself at home in your life, immediately beginning the remodeling process necessary for Christ to be seen in every aspect of your life. From that point on, your salvation is secure. Regardless of how sin-stained or sin-wrecked your life is when you entrust it to Christ, all is forgiven. However, you have a ruthless enemy who is determined to thwart God's renovation plans for your life by any means possible and keep you from telling anyone else the Good News.

If you are a Christian, you can "walk in the light as He [Jesus Christ] is in the light" (1 John 1:7a). This power is available in the Holy Spirit, who is always with the Christian. Living the Christian life—walking in the light—is only possible by continually agreeing with the truth He reveals and letting Him exchange, change, and rearrange however He sees fit. The truth is found in the Bible. The Christian life is nurtured in your personal devotional life of Bible study and prayer but expressed in your relationships—both with your brothers and sisters in Christ and with non-Christians.

Until Jesus returns, the physical lives of Christians will end but not without hope. The resurrection of Jesus validates His promise of eternal life to those who follow Him. New life in Christ is best lived with the end in mind (see 2 Pet. 3), not only looking forward to God's justice and the rewards of endurance but also looking for opportunities to proclaim the gospel (see 1 Pet. 4). From confession of faith into eternity, the new life in Christ is a reflection of Christ Himself, an extension of His work in the world, and a witness of salvation to those who are unsaved.

Blessings,
Rhonda Kelley

A Pattern of Personal Quiet Time

The commitment to building intimacy with the Lord Jesus is personal—not something anyone else can build into your life. Whether a child, teenager, young adult, or mature woman—whether you are new in your faith journey or spiritually strong and disciplined in your faith, you must initiate genuine, heart-felt communication with the Lord and establish your own pattern for sustaining the relationship you have established with the Lord Jesus.

Women throughout history—from Bible times to the current generation—have been marked by such a commitment. The maidservant of Naaman's wife was taken from her parents into captivity at a young age (2 Kings 5:1–3); yet she had already developed a relationship with the living God. She kept her faith; she shared it. Her strength did not come because of many years of spiritual training but because she started at a young age and refused to let earthly circumstances destroy a heavenly commitment. The Moabitess Ruth had no witness to the true God until after she married, but she observed her mother-in-law Naomi and learned spiritual disciplines, which brought her into a relationship with the living God and introduced her to the joys of serving Him.

This commitment to hearing and knowing God's Word and then living it out in practical ways (see Matt. 7:24) thrives and blooms in the presence of the Lord—reading His Word, listening for His voice, sharing your innermost fears and petitions, spending quality as well as quantity time with Him.

Women more than anything else need a word from God. The written Word of God was prepared in "the fullness of the time" (Gal. 4:4) and continues to speak to women in every season of life with the same authority and clarity throughout the generations. Scripture does not speak in detail to every situation in life, but the Bible records timeless principles that continue to be timely solutions to all of life's challenges.

The Devotional for Women is a tool for you to use in pursuing your spiritual journey with purpose and passion, putting yourself in the presence of the Lord for a time of prayer and reading His Word.

Woman-to-woman devotionals will add an inspirational thought or instructive moment to your time with the Lord. Now this companion journal will offer an option beyond space for brief reflection. Journaling is the way to record your spiritual journey. Through the years I have kept many different journals. Putting my gratitude to God into words, recording blessings and answered prayers for praise now and in the future is great therapy for responding to future doubts and frustrations, questions and anxieties. Only God and my journal really know the depths of my despair, the heat of my anger, and the pit of depression into which I can fall. Journals can become a personal "life file"—detailing and keeping track of the highlights and personal events of life recorded in an orderly and organized fashion.

Sit at the Lord's feet, read His Word, meditate on its application to life, pour out your praise and petition to Him! Do this every day, and consider making a commitment to work through the entire year with a pattern of personal quiet time devoted to pursuing the Lord—not through an ordinary ritual but rather establishing an extraordinary life discipline that will carry you through life with purpose and praise. Hopefully this journal will provide another tool for uninterrupted and focused time with the Lord.

Dorothy Kelley Patterson

God intentionally created the man and the woman as distinct yet complementary beings.
(Gen. 1:27; 2:18)

God had a beautiful and specific purpose in mind when He created Eve—she was to be a "helper" for Adam. (Gen. 2:18, 20)

Marriage was established as one man and one woman in a lifetime commitment. (Gen. 2:24–25)

A mother is God's channel for spiritual nurture. (Prov. 1:8)

Strive to make your home a sanctuary—
not merely providing shelter but peace,
rest, and joy. (Prov. 31:27)

Nothing brings more beauty to person
and life than the love of Christ within—
it literally bursts out. (Prov. 30:31)

God created me and you according to His design to make a difference in this world. (Eph. 2:10)

Christian marriages are to be witnesses to lost people, reflecting the way Christ loves the church. (Eph. 5:32)

Mentoring relationships among women were ordained by God as a profoundly effective way to transfer from generation to generation biblical instruction and spiritual applications.

(Titus 2:3–5)

Biblical submission is willingly choosing to obey, voluntarily placing yourself under the authority of another. (1 Pet. 3:1–2)

Your outward appearance is merely the frame around the life's message emanating from within your heart. (1 Pet. 3:3–4)

Those who refresh others will themselves be refreshed. (Prov. 11:25)

Make faith your first response and not your last resort. (Heb. 11:1)

Faith does not take you around storms, but it will carry you through! (James 1:2–4)

Beware of worry: it does not solve tomorrow's problems, but it does rob today of its joys. (Phil. 4:6–7)

The way you live your life offers a greater legacy than the words you say. (James 1:22)

Daily Bible Reading Plan

Daily Bible reading plans have been developed to familiarize readers with God's Word through a systematic reading of portions of Scripture every day. Many different daily Bible reading plans are available to assist Christians in developing the spiritual discipline of Bible study. This unique plan follows these devotional readings from Genesis to Revelation providing the broader biblical context and insight into the whole counsel of truth.

DAY	SCRIPTURE
□ 1	Genesis 1—3
□ 2	Genesis 4—6
□ 3	Genesis 7—10
□ 4	Genesis 11—13
□ 5	Genesis 14—16
□ 6	Genesis 17—20
□ 7	Genesis 21—23
□ 8	Genesis 24—26
□ 9	Genesis 27—29
□ 10	Genesis 30—32
□ 11	Genesis 33—35
□ 12	Genesis 36—38
□ 13	Genesis 39—41
□ 14	Genesis 42—44
□ 15	Genesis 45—47
□ 16	Genesis 48—50
□ 17	Exodus 1—7
□ 18	Exodus 8—14
□ 19	Exodus 15—20
□ 20	Exodus 21—27
□ 21	Exodus 28—33
□ 22	Exodus 34—40
□ 23	Leviticus 1—7
□ 24	Leviticus 8—14

□ 25 . . . . Leviticus 15—21
□ 26 . . . . Leviticus 22—27
□ 27 . . . . Numbers 1—9
□ 28 . . . . Numbers 10—19
□ 29 . . . . Numbers 20—28
□ 30 . . . . Numbers 29—36
□ 31 . . . . Deuteronomy 1—6
□ 32 . . . . Deuteronomy 7—14
□ 33 . . . . Deuteronomy 15—20
□ 34 . . . . Deuteronomy 21—27
□ 35 . . . . Deuteronomy 28—34
□ 36 . . . . Joshua 1—4
□ 37 . . . . Joshua 5—8
□ 38 . . . . Joshua 9—12
□ 39 . . . . Joshua 13—16
□ 40 . . . . Joshua 17—20
□ 41 . . . . Joshua 21—24
□ 42 . . . . Judges 1—2
□ 43 . . . . Judges 3—4
□ 44 . . . . Judges 5—6
□ 45 . . . . Judges 7—8
□ 46 . . . . Judges 9—10
□ 47 . . . . Judges 11—12
□ 48 . . . . Judges 13—14
□ 49 . . . . Judges 14—15
□ 50 . . . . Judges 16—17
□ 51 . . . . Judges 18—19
□ 52 . . . . Judges 20
□ 53 . . . . Judges 21
□ 54 . . . . Ruth 1:1–10
□ 55 . . . . Ruth 1:11–22
□ 56 . . . . Ruth 2:1–16
□ 57 . . . . Ruth 2:17–23
□ 58 . . . . Ruth 3:1–9
□ 59 . . . . Ruth 3:10–18
□ 60 . . . . Ruth 4:1–22

□ 61 . . . . 1 Samuel 1—4
□ 62 . . . . 1 Samuel 5—7
□ 63 . . . . 1 Samuel 8—11
□ 64 . . . . 1 Samuel 12—14
□ 65 . . . . 1 Samuel 15—17
□ 66 . . . . 1 Samuel 18—22
□ 67 . . . . 1 Samuel 23—25
□ 68 . . . . 1 Samuel 26—28
□ 69 . . . . 1 Samuel 29—31
□ 70 . . . . 2 Samuel 1—3
□ 71 . . . . 2 Samuel 4—6
□ 72 . . . . 2 Samuel 7—8
□ 73 . . . . 2 Samuel 9—10
□ 74 . . . . 2 Samuel 11—12
□ 75 . . . . 2 Samuel 13—15
□ 76 . . . . 2 Samuel 16—18
□ 77 . . . . 2 Samuel 19—21
□ 78 . . . . 2 Samuel 22—24
□ 79 . . . . 1 Kings 1—3
□ 80 . . . . 1 Kings 4—6
□ 81 . . . . 1 Kings 7—9
□ 82 . . . . 1 Kings 10—12
□ 83 . . . . 1 Kings 13—15
□ 84 . . . . 1 Kings 16—18
□ 85 . . . . 1 Kings 19—22
□ 86 . . . . 2 Kings 1—4
□ 87 . . . . 2 Kings 5—8
□ 88 . . . . 2 Kings 9—12
□ 89 . . . . 2 Kings 13—16
□ 90 . . . . 2 Kings 17—20
□ 91 . . . . 2 Kings 21—25
□ 92 . . . . 1 Chronicles 1—10
□ 93 . . . . 1 Chronicles 11—20
□ 94 . . . . 1 Chronicles 21—29
□ 95 . . . . 2 Chronicles 1—9
□ 96 . . . . 2 Chronicles 10—19

□ 97 . . . . 2 Chronicles 20—29
□ 98 . . . . 2 Chronicles 30—36
□ 99 . . . . Ezra 1—5
□ 100 . . . . Ezra 6—10
□ 101. . . . . Nehemiah 1—4
□ 102 . . . . Nehemiah 5—8
□ 103 . . . . Nehemiah 9—13
□ 104 . . . . Esther 1—4
□ 105 . . . . Esther 5—7
□ 106 . . . . Esther 8—10
□ 107 . . . . Job 1—6
□ 108 . . . . Job 7—12
□ 109 . . . . Job 13—18
□ 110. . . . . Job 19—24
□ 111. . . . . Job 25—30
□ 112 . . . . Job 31—37
□ 113 . . . . Job 38—42
□ 114. . . . . Psalms 1—10
□ 115 . . . . Psalms 11—20
□ 116. . . . . Psalms 21—30
□ 117. . . . . Psalms 31—40
□ 118 . . . . Psalms 41—50
□ 119 . . . . Psalms 51—61
□ 120 . . . . Psalms 62—69
□ 121 . . . . Psalms 70—77
□ 122 . . . . Psalms 78—83
□ 123 . . . . Psalms 84—91
□ 124 . . . . Psalms 92—99
□ 125 . . . . Psalms 100—110
□ 126 . . . . Psalms 111—118
□ 127 . . . . Psalm 119
□ 128 . . . . Psalms 120—127
□ 129 . . . . Psalms 128—138
□ 130 . . . . Psalms 139—145
□ 131 . . . . Psalms 146—150
□ 132 . . . . Proverbs 1—3

□ 133 . . . . Proverbs 4—6
□ 134 . . . . Proverbs 7—9
□ 135 . . . . Proverbs 10—12
□ 136 . . . . Proverbs 13—15
□ 137 . . . . Proverbs 16—18
□ 138 . . . . Proverbs 19—21
□ 139 . . . . Proverbs 22—24
□ 140 . . . . Proverbs 25—27
□ 141. . . . . Proverbs 28—30
□ 142 . . . . Proverbs 31:1–9
□ 143 . . . . Proverbs 31:10–31
□ 144 . . . . Ecclesiastes 1—2
□ 145 . . . . Ecclesiastes 3—4
□ 146 . . . . Ecclesiastes 5—6
□ 147. . . . . Ecclesiastes 7—10
□ 148 . . . . Ecclesiastes 11—12
□ 149 . . . . Song of Solomon 1—2
□ 150 . . . . Song of Solomon 3—4
□ 151 . . . . Song of Solomon 5—6
□ 152 . . . . Song of Solomon 7—8
□ 153 . . . . Isaiah 1—6
□ 154 . . . . Isaiah 7—12
□ 155 . . . . Isaiah 13—18
□ 156 . . . . Isaiah 19—24
□ 157 . . . . Isaiah 25—30
□ 158 . . . . Isaiah 31—36
□ 159 . . . . Isaiah 37—42
□ 160 . . . . Isaiah 43—48
□ 161. . . . . Isaiah 49—54
□ 162 . . . . Isaiah 55—60
□ 163 . . . . Isaiah 61—66
□ 164 . . . . Jeremiah 1—7
□ 165 . . . . Jeremiah 8—14
□ 166 . . . . Jeremiah 15—23
□ 167 . . . . Jeremiah 24—30
□ 168 . . . . Jeremiah 31—37

□ 169 . . . . Jeremiah 38—44
□ 170. . . . . Jeremiah 45—52
□ 171 . . . . Lamentations 1—3
□ 172 . . . . Lamentations 4—5
□ 173 . . . . Ezekiel 1—12
□ 174. . . . . Ezekiel 13—24
□ 175 . . . . Ezekiel 25—36
□ 176. . . . . Ezekiel 37—48
□ 177 . . . . Daniel 1—2
□ 178. . . . . Daniel 3—5
□ 179 . . . . Daniel 6—7
□ 180 . . . . Daniel 8—10
□ 181 . . . . Daniel 11—12
□ 182 . . . . Hosea 1—5
□ 183 . . . . Hosea 6—10
□ 184 . . . . Hosea 11—14
□ 185 . . . . Joel 1
□ 186 . . . . Joel 2—3
□ 187 . . . . Amos 1—2
□ 188 . . . . Amos 3—4
□ 189 . . . . Amos 5—6
□ 190 . . . . Amos 7—9
□ 191 . . . . Obadiah 1–21
□ 192 . . . . Jonah 1
□ 193 . . . . Jonah 2
□ 194 . . . . Jonah 3
□ 195 . . . . Jonah 4
□ 196 . . . . Micah 1—2
□ 197 . . . . Micah 3—4
□ 198 . . . . Micah 5—6
□ 199 . . . . Micah 7
□ 200 . . . . Nahum 1
□ 201 . . . . Nahum 2
□ 202 . . . . Nahum 3
□ 203 . . . . Habakkuk 1
□ 204 . . . . Habakkuk 2

□ 205 . . . . Habakkuk 3
□ 206 . . . . Zephaniah 1—2
□ 207 . . . . Zephaniah 3
□ 208 . . . . Haggai 1
□ 209 . . . . Haggai 2
□ 210. . . . . Zechariah 1—5
□ 211. . . . . Zechariah 6—10
□ 212 . . . . Zechariah 11—14
□ 213 . . . . Malachi 1—2
□ 214. . . . . Malachi 3
□ 215 . . . . Malachi 4
□ 216. . . . . Matthew 1—2
□ 217. . . . . Matthew 3—4
□ 218 . . . . Matthew 5
□ 219 . . . . Matthew 6
□ 220 . . . . Matthew 7
□ 221 . . . . Matthew 8—9
□ 222 . . . . Matthew 10—12
□ 223 . . . . Matthew 13—14
□ 224 . . . . Matthew 15—16
□ 225 . . . . Matthew 17—18
□ 226 . . . . Matthew 19—21
□ 227 . . . . Matthew 22—23
□ 228 . . . . Matthew 24—25
□ 229 . . . . Matthew 26
□ 230 . . . . Matthew 27
□ 231 . . . . Matthew 28
□ 232 . . . . Mark 1—4
□ 233 . . . . Mark 5—7
□ 234 . . . . Mark 8—10
□ 235 . . . . Mark 11—13
□ 236 . . . . Mark 14—16
□ 237 . . . . Luke 1
□ 238 . . . . Luke 2—3
□ 239 . . . . Luke 4—6
□ 240 . . . . Luke 7—9

□ 241 . . . . Luke 10—12
□ 242 . . . . Luke 13—16
□ 243 . . . . Luke 17—19
□ 244 . . . . Luke 20—22
□ 245 . . . . Luke 23—24
□ 246 . . . . John 1—4
□ 247 . . . . John 5—8
□ 248 . . . . John 9—12
□ 249 . . . . John 13—15
□ 250 . . . . John 16—21
□ 251 . . . . Acts 1—3
□ 252 . . . . Acts 4—6
□ 253 . . . . Acts 7—9
□ 254 . . . . Acts 10—12
□ 255 . . . . Acts 13—15
□ 256 . . . . Acts 16—18
□ 257 . . . . Acts 19—20
□ 258 . . . . Acts 21—22
□ 259 . . . . Acts 23—24
□ 260 . . . . Acts 25—28
□ 261 . . . . Romans 1—2
□ 262 . . . . Romans 3—4
□ 263 . . . . Romans 5—6
□ 264 . . . . Romans 7—8
□ 265 . . . . Romans 9—10
□ 266 . . . . Romans 11—12
□ 267 . . . . Romans 13—14
□ 268 . . . . Romans 15—16
□ 269 . . . . 1 Corinthians 1
□ 270 . . . . 1 Corinthians 2—3
□ 271 . . . . 1 Corinthians 4
□ 272 . . . . 1 Corinthians 5—6
□ 273 . . . . 1 Corinthians 7
□ 274 . . . . 1 Corinthians 8—9
□ 275 . . . . 1 Corinthians 10—11
□ 276 . . . . 1 Corinthians 12

□ 277 . . . . 1 Corinthians 13
□ 278 . . . . 1 Corinthians 14
□ 279 . . . . 1 Corinthians 15—16
□ 280 . . . . 2 Corinthians 1—2
□ 281 . . . . 2 Corinthians 3—4
□ 282 . . . . 2 Corinthians 5—6
□ 283 . . . . 2 Corinthians 7—8
□ 284 . . . . 2 Corinthians 9—10
□ 285 . . . . 2 Corinthians 11—13
□ 286 . . . . Galatians 1
□ 287 . . . . Galatians 2
□ 288 . . . . Galatians 3
□ 289 . . . . Galatians 4
□ 290 . . . . Galatians 5:1–15
□ 291 . . . . Galatians 5:16–26
□ 292 . . . . Galatians 6
□ 293 . . . . Ephesians 1
□ 294 . . . . Ephesians 2
□ 295 . . . . Ephesians 3
□ 296 . . . . Ephesians 4
□ 297 . . . . Ephesians 5
□ 298 . . . . Ephesians 6
□ 299 . . . . Philippians 1
□ 300 . . . . Philippians 2
□ 301 . . . . Philippians 3:1–10
□ 302 . . . . Philippians 3:11–21
□ 303 . . . . Philippians 4:1–6
□ 304 . . . . Philippians 4:7–13
□ 305 . . . . Philippians 4:14–33
□ 306 . . . . Colossians 1—2
□ 307 . . . . Colossians 3—4
□ 308 . . . . 1 Thessalonians 1—2
□ 309 . . . . 1 Thessalonians 3—4
□ 310. . . . . 1 Thessalonians 5
□ 311. . . . . 2 Thessalonians 1—2
□ 312 . . . . 2 Thessalonians 3

□ 313 . . . . 1 Timothy 1
□ 314. . . . . 1 Timothy 2
□ 315 . . . . 1 Timothy 3
□ 316. . . . . 1 Timothy 4
□ 317. . . . . 1 Timothy 5
□ 318. . . . . 1 Timothy 6
□ 319 . . . . 2 Timothy 1
□ 320 . . . . 2 Timothy 2
□ 321 . . . . 2 Timothy 3
□ 322 . . . . 2 Timothy 4
□ 323 . . . . Titus 1
□ 324 . . . . Titus 2
□ 325 . . . . Titus 3
□ 326 . . . . Philemon 1–16
□ 327 . . . . Philemon 17–25
□ 328 . . . . Hebrews 1—3
□ 329 . . . . Hebrews 4—6
□ 330 . . . . Hebrews 7—9
□ 331 . . . . Hebrews 10—13
□ 332 . . . . James 1:1–20
□ 333 . . . . James 1:21–27
□ 334 . . . . James 2:1–13
□ 335 . . . . James 2:14–26
□ 336 . . . . James 3
□ 337 . . . . James 4
□ 338 . . . . James 5
□ 339 . . . . 1 Peter 1
□ 340 . . . . 1 Peter 2:1–12
□ 341 . . . . 1 Peter 2:13–25
□ 342 . . . . 1 Peter 3
□ 343 . . . . 1 Peter 4
□ 344 . . . . 1 Peter 5
□ 345 . . . . 2 Peter 1
□ 346 . . . . 2 Peter 2
□ 347 . . . . 2 Peter 3
□ 348 . . . . 1 John 1

□ 349 . . . . 1 John 2
□ 350 . . . . 1 John 3
□ 351 . . . . 1 John 4
□ 352 . . . . 1 John 5:1–13
□ 353 . . . . 1 John 5:14–21
□ 354 . . . . 2 John 1–13
□ 355 . . . . 3 John 1–14
□ 356 . . . . Jude 1–25
□ 357 . . . . Revelation 1—2
□ 358 . . . . Revelation 3—4
□ 359 . . . . Revelation 5—6
□ 360 . . . . Revelation 7—8
□ 361 . . . . Revelation 9—11
□ 362 . . . . Revelation 12—14
□ 363 . . . . Revelation 15—17
□ 364 . . . . Revelation 18—20
□ 365 . . . . Revelation 21
□ 366 . . . . Revelation 22

Co-Editors

Rhonda Harrington Kelley is the president's wife and adjunct professor of women's ministry at New Orleans Baptist Theological Seminary. She is also a Christian author and speaker. Formerly the director of speech pathology at Ochsner Medical Center, Dr. Kelley has a Master of Arts in Speech Pathology from Baylor University, a Doctor of Philosophy in Special Education from University of New Orleans, and additional studies in Women's Ministry from New Orleans Baptist Theological Seminary. She lives in New Orleans, Louisiana, with her husband Chuck, who has been president of New Orleans Baptist Theological Seminary since 1996.

Dorothy Kelley Patterson, a homemaker, helps her husband Paige Patterson, president of Southwestern Baptist Theological Seminary, by serving as professor of theology in women's studies. With graduate and post-graduate degrees in theology, Dr. Patterson teaches, speaks, and writes for women. She is a member of the Evangelical Theological Society; she was a founding member of the Council for Biblical Manhood and Womanhood; she is a member of Birchman Baptist Church. The Pattersons reside in Fort Worth, Texas, but travel extensively throughout the world. Their children Armour and Rachel Patterson, as well as Carmen and Mark Howell with their daughters Abigail and Rebekah, live in Texas.

More Resources from Dorothy Kelley Patterson & Rhonda Harrington Kelley

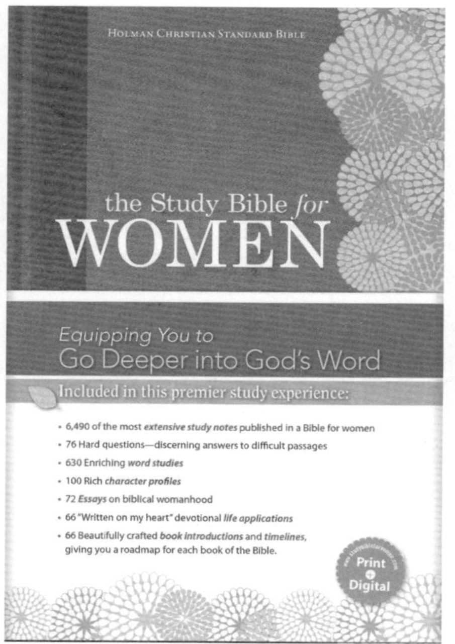

In *The Study Bible for Women*, you will join a host of other women, all academically trained in the original languages of the Bible and passionate about God's Word, for an intimately deep dive into Scripture that will equip you to unlock the riches and majesty of His Word, and ignite a passion to mentor others in your life to do the same.

The Devotional for Women provides a solution to a problem that nearly all women have—how to be more faithful to read God's Word and know how to apply it to their lives.

The *Women's Evangelical Commentaries* are written and edited by women for women. While other commentaries take an egalitarian view of the relationship between men and women, the editors and writers of these commentaries believe the complementarian view of the relationship between men and women most accurately interprets God's intent as expressed in Scripture.